and enduring interest, while the subject is temporarily of pressing importance.

On the present occasion I shall confine myself to the question which immediately interests the public, and which I have undertaken to answer. I shall chiefly state facts, and endeavour to establish a principle which will elucidate the cause of the failure, and point out the way to improvement. Into all possible consequences which imagination may conceive, a whole life would not suffice to inquire; and I must respectfully request you not to allow the glare of some supposed future danger to conceal the pitfalls which now lie immediately in the path of society. My answer to the question, "What shall we do with our criminals?" is "Don't create them," and my object is to show that our criminals are the inevitable results of an erroneous system, relieving the wisdom of Nature and the governed people from the blame of the vast criminality now wholly and exclusively, and with much conceit, thrown on them.

I am not to speak of ticket-of-leave men nor juvenile criminality, nor this petty improvement in gaol discipline, nor that new system of transportation, but to take an enlarged, and philosophical view; and I must begin by reminding you that the subject is wholly psychological. Penalties are inflicted on the body, but the pain which results, the emotions, the motives sought to be produced, are entirely mental. To each individual's own consciousness these are very familiar phenomena; in relation to their causes they are amongst the mysteries of creation. The chasm between an infliction on the body and the resulting state of consciousness science has not bridged over nor art filled up so as to ensure the certain passage and transmutation of the bodily infliction into the mental emotion we desire. How very little we know of what is passing in each others mind is a common remark; but we never know what another feels as we know what we see and handle. From our own recollections and impressions, we may make shrewd guesses at what others feel; but these guesses are our feelings not theirs, and it is as impossible to know the feelings and thoughts of another as to weigh the distant star, the light from which has just reached the earth.

The difference between the impression made on different

individuals by the same object becomes apparent, when we reflect on all which the cultivated eye of a Ruskin, or the long-gathered knowledge of an Owen, perceives at once in every object brought before it, from a tuft of grass to a rainbow, from a creeping slug to some great Saurian reptile, or to man himself, the lord of the creation. We can have no doubt that in the minds of such, and of all cultivated men, the mental effect of every object beheld is different from that which the same object produces in a superstitious Hindoo or a Hottentot. The vast difference between the impressions on the mind of the savage and the civilized man is entirely the consequence of previous states of mind. Countless evanescent, observations and remarks, and some durable sensations and emotions, not merely of the two cultivated individuals, but of the many cultivated men who preceded them in the paths of criticism on art and of natural science, and who contributed to form their taste or enlarge their knowledge, make up the difference. A civilized man is the possessor of a glorious inheritance of mind accumulated through ages, though the mass of materials which went to form it have, like many other creations in every part of nature, been allowed to perish. The scaffolding is removed, but the building is all the more simple and magnificent. The materials only existed in consciousness, and have, like the spring blossoms which are the harbinger of fruit, for ever disappeared. In all other human beings, as in these examples of extreme and peculiar cultivation, preformed associations, experience gathered in their own lives and by their predecessors, and transmitted to them, give to each one peculiar idiosyncracies, which lend their own tints and forms to every object beheld. The media of perception, whether organs of sense or nerves, exhibit no differences corresponding to the different mental results in different individuals. This, then, is a mysterious part of our nature.

> " In following life through creatures we dissect,
> We lose it at the moment we detect."

Nevertheless, the fact that feelings and thoughts are communicated from mind to mind is certain. How a smile in a mother causes joy in an infant, and calls forth its answering smile, though very familiar is not explained by philosophy. How a few marks on paper excite in cultivated minds thoughts and sentiments something like those which inspired

Homer's tongue, or can excite at one and the same time similar emotions in Melbourne and London, in New York and Houg Kong; or how the character and conduct of Queen Elizabeth and Charles II. influence the minds of this generation, is only to be explained by saying the fact is so. Not knowing the philosophy of this fact, we do not know how to direct the influence which one mind exercises over another, and which all minds exercise over each; and we can never be sure what will be the feelings our conduct and language may excite in others. But on this influence of mind over mind depends the whole theory of punishment and education. He who supposes that the pain he inflicts on the body, or the precept he dins into the ear will infallibly be transmuted into that state of mind which he wishes to produce, must be blind to experience, and has yet to learn the first elements of mental science and of penal jurisprudence.

That you may not expect immediate advantages, which cannot accrue from any teaching, I must remind you that all action on penal laws must be national, and all that a reasonable man can hope is to correct opinion, leaving practical improvements to time. No individual, however earnest his convictions, and urgent the necessity may appear to give them effect, is entitled to expect or require that they should be the impulse and immediate guide to legislation. Only practical men, so called, who "rush in where angels fear to tread," propose, and very often succeed in enacting laws from their own crude fancies. In the end, we know that "action" will "take the path," in which opinion says "it follows good or flees from evil;" but national action should be the remote consequence of opinion first necessarily promulgated by some one mind, and gradually shared by others. The sentiments which precede it may have been slowly formed through ages, though the expression of them may have been continually smothered, only to make them more powerful in the end, when they manifest themselves in some great national change. Then legislation may be the proper expression for them; but individuals, however enlightened or wise, are not justified in making their convictions the rules for other men.

To meet some objections which have already been made to what I have written, and forestall others, allow me to remind you of the great and unanticipated changes, both in principles of government and modes of thought, both material and moral, which in modern times have taken place, followed only by beneficial consequences. The ruin of society has been predicted from the melioration of our criminal code, which was begun about 1809, from the abolition of restrictions on commerce, from the extensive use of machinery, and from the progress of luxury, from all which nothing but advantages have accrued. The moderns have worked out a science of the material world, a philosophy of mechanics, and a series of wonderful arts of which the wisest nations of antiquity had no conception. But while we should look with contempt on the most splendid chariot that ever secured for a victor the crown of the Olympic games, as the clumsy contrivance of ignorance, in comparison with our steam-dragged cars, we still regard the Greeks and other nations of antiquity as our guides in moral and political science. Except as necessity has driven us gradually to adapt old laws to modern growth, institutions, especially penal laws, are based on principles similar to those adopted in the earliest stages of civilisation. Our theory of punishment dates from the most remote antiquity—our recognised philosophy of mechanics is scarcely two centuries old. Every day we behold as fruits of the latter, brilliant achievements far surpassing the expectations of the most florid imagination, and every day we have to condemn and sweep away, as at variance with actual existence, the logical and established deductions from the former. No departure, therefore, let me suggest, from our present system however extreme, no contradiction to received principles of government however great, ought, merely on this account, now to be regarded as strange, or classed as presumptuous.

All crimes are not the result of our systems. There exists in man a conviction that he is bound to perform some, and to abstain from performing other, actions ; and every deed at variance with this conviction, from the most flagitious matricide to the smallest theft, is properly regarded and classed as a crime. Antecedently to all governments, and co-existing with all governments, whatever their nature, man commits grievous offences, and he would not be man fallible and ignorant, yet aspiring to be good and wise, were he not, whatever be the effects of human laws, liable to be criminal. But of the universal liability to do wrong—common to all classes, in all ages, and in all places, shared by the lawgiver and the population—curious as it appears when reflected on, though it is neccessarily mentioned, it is not my intention to discourse. I acknowledge its existence as characteristic of human nature, not the result of human laws, but not to be got rid of by them, or by any human contrivance. I shall first call your attention to certain well-known but leading facts concerning the crimes punished by our laws.

The number of commitments for trial in England and Wales (confining our attention to one part of the Empire) was, in 1854, the latest year of which the official accounts were published when this lecture was prepared—(those of 1855 have since been published, but they supply no reason for altering my remarks)—the number of commitments in England and Wales, in 1854, was 29,359, an increase of 8.8 per cent. on the previous year. "This increase, it is some satisfaction," says the compiler of the returns, "to be able to state is *confined to the least grave class of offences*, and OFFENCES OF VIOLENCE HAVE, ON THE WHOLE, decreased." "*The offences against property, without violence, comprise about four-fifths of the indictable crimes*, and, in this large class, the increase of 11 per cent. shows how largely the increase of commitments in the year is made up of offences of *the least grave character*."

This official description of the national criminality in 1854, is applicable, with one or two brief exceptions, to the whole period between 1805, when our criminal records were first kept with some but not sufficient care, and 1843.

"These returns are now any thing," says Mr Hill, the recorder of Birmingham, "but full, and, I fear, anything but accurate." Complicated, confused, and inaccurate as they still are, till 1805 the legislature took no pains to learn the consequences of its own acts, and the effects of imprisoning, transporting, and hanging our fellow-creatures, which it ordered, were, till that time, whatever might be supposed, actually hidden from the public eye.

Since 1805, we are informed by these imperfect official returns, that, except three periods of interruption—from 1821 to 1825, from 1834 to 1837, and from 1843, when a great many restrictions on commerce were removed, to 1853—in all which periods there was comparative plenty in the land, the number of commitments has gone on, as in 1854, increasing. The average of the three years, 1805-7, was 4,466 ; the average of the three years, 1852-54, was 27,975, a "frightful increase" of more than six fold, while the population, in the interval, had only increased about 90 per cent. This would be terribly alarmimg both for the present and the future, but for the fact, that the continual increase has been always confined, as in 1854, to the "least grave class of offences." Great and serious crimes have continually diminished.

"The increase in commitments," said Mr. Porter, in 1842, is chiefly in offences committed against property without violence." At that period, these offences constituted 79.31 hundredths of the whole ; in 1854, they had increased to 81.12 hundredths. Thus, *the great majority of all the crimes punished by the law* after a solemn trial, excluding all summary convictions—more than four-fifths of all the offences the increase of which so alarms the community, *are offences against property committed without violence.* They are vulgar, low, mean plunder. Nationally speaking, we are conspicuous for pilfering, not for assassination. The proportion of these offences against property is continually augmenting, while the graver and more atrocious crimes are, on the whole, continually diminishing. Most of these graver crimes, too, originate in a desire for property, as burglaries, garottings, some poisonings, and other murders.

Do not run away, I beseech you, with the notion, because the police reports were lately full of deeds of violence—the results, probably—as far as they are now more numerous than formerly—of the deeds of violence, and the great increase of taxation, we have all lately encouraged by our demands for war—do not run away with the notion that such deeds are continually on the increase. A comprehensive view assures us that the fact, happily is, as I have stated, that crimes of violence are, on the whole, and in the long run, continually decreasing.

Nor is this remarkable change unexampled in other countries. Though the progress towards a diminution of violent crimes is more rapid in England than in France, as was ascertained long ago, still a similar progress is taking place there. "The old crimes, by the old methods, against persons," says M. Dupont White, a late writer, "and against property are diminishing. On the contrary, there is a notable increase in certain crimes which have only been met by modern laws, such as fraud, bankruptcy, false money, abuses of trust, extortion of titles and signatures, &c. Offences," he concludes, "become less serious and more numerous." The diminution of violence, then, is a general fact, the causes of which it behoves legislators to study. I shall only say that it is in no degree owing to the preservation of the gallows here and the erection of the guillotine there. The lazy veneration of capital punishments, still inculcated by men in office, is now shared by very few reflecting persons beyond the official circle, and by the most unthinking vulgar, whom the official example influences. The old barbarity is continued much more from habit than from a general and rational conviction of its utility.

The progress mentioned I regard as thoroughly established, and as lying at the basis of all just reasoning on the effects of penal laws. Crimes of violence, including wars, to repeat the important statement, have continuously and successively decreased, and the *increase* of crimes recorded in our criminal returns is wholly of crimes against property. This important fact may relieve timid doubters of all anxiety as to the future of society; it limits my remarks to one class of offences. To show how our system creates criminals, I have only to show how it induces theft.

I wish first to remind you of the great influence which men, by their conduct, as well as by their words, exercise over one another. This general principle seems to me extremely efficacious in moulding character, and to be provided for the very purpose of easily inciting others to do all that we wish them to do, which is all that we can require from all the punishments that ingenuity can devise and cruelty inflict. If I am successful in conveying to you my impressions on this matter, you will find no difficulty, even should I not, in a second lecture, have an opportunity of shewing, in detail, the operation of our laws, in ascertaining for yourselves how the crimes we punish in vain are caused. I make no claim like persons armed with authority, to say that you must not do this, or must not do that; I only say that doing this or doing that certain consequences follow inevitably, which are evil or good, and it is for the public to choose betwixt them.

Example is emphatically said to be better than precept, and I might have contented myself with mentioning the fact, and have passed on to point out how the example of the upper classes, especially the legislating classes, dealing with all property as if it belonged to them, generates crimes against property; but this familiar fact is not, as the exponent of a general principle, so forcibly impressed on the public mind as to make it safe to rely on it as the basis of a great argument. Dr. Paley, and other writers, have recognised the influence of imitation in diffusing amongst mankind similar behaviour and similar sentiments. He says, "if any thing in children deserves the name of an instinct, it is their propensity to imitation." But, as far as I recollect, he makes no further use of the principle, and does not show how by its means the example of a revered or respected authority becomes, whatever may be said or taught, or decreed to the contrary, the model on which other men are formed. This is what I shall endeavour to illustrate.

"Tell me your company," says the proverb, "and I will tell you what you are." The mutual influence of criminals and the mutual corruption engendered by shutting them up unclassified to herd with each other are always recognised; but the influence which makes *them* like one another, or assimilates them all to a common standard is in principle the same as the influence of good society, which moulds all the frequenters of the saloons of Belgravia into the forms which are the fashions of the season.

Poets and novelists continually point out with equal truth and earnestness the holy influence of some quiet, unobtrusive, yet always diligent, and always kind mother, aunt, sister, or friend, over the character and welfare of a family. Such examples of individual influence, including cases where the effects are totally opposite, and of an unholy character, must have fallen under every man's observation. This influence, powerful in families, must be powerful in nations made up of families. If it do not thunder in the streets, nor flash through congregations of busy men, though in them it sometimes rouses a general feeling that may be mutinous or heroic, it makes up for an apparent want of power and intensity by percolating through every stratum of society and carrying something of the properties of each to all. "Each living soul," says a writer to me unknown, "has its influence on others, in some way and to some extent; consciously or unconsciously one mind colours another; a child acts on children; servants upon their fellow-servants; masters on those they employ; parents on their children; friends on friends. Even when we do not design to influence others, our manner of life, our conversation, our deeds, are all the while having weight somewhere or somehow; our feet leave the impression, though we may not look behind us to see the marks."

Another proverb says, "one fool makes many." The generalisation is just. What monstrosities of dress, what vain dull amusements, what trifling similar occupations, originating we hardly know how, are adopted by both sexes. An exalted lady, in a peculiar condition, conceals the change in her shape, and immediately all the fashionable maidens jump into hoops and flounces, and hide their forms as completely as the grub hides the butterfly. A man of high station, prematurely bald, covers his head with a frizzled peruke, and all his courtiers, all the high-bred people in his own and other lands, hide their natural hair under unsightly nasty greasy wigs. Count Bruhl, chief minister of Saxony when it was, a century ago, more powerful than at present, had some 170 perukes, and each was part of a full dress which was not complete without a cane. He and his master avowedly imitated Louis XIV., for a long period the master-modist or man-milliner of Europe. Frederick the Great, a modist of a sterner character, whose impress might be perceived in Germany in peasants' dresses long after the battle of Jena, the forerunner, too, of a greater but not sterner military modist, nipped the glory of Saxony and of Count Bruhl. The monarch expressed his astonishment that a man without a head should have so many wigs. But in his sense of wanting a head—that is, wanting sagacity and humanity, you will probably think the great king himself, and his brother modists, when they wasted the produce of industry and the substance of the people in idle pomp or worse war, were not more gifted with heads than Count Bruhl.

The generalisation exemplified by the conduct of the courts of Europe in imitating Louis XIV., is, however, true of wise men as well as fools. What crowds of inventors of poets and novelists are called into existence by the example of one great success. If it be wisdom to make the multitude religious and moral by education, and improve them by art exhibitions, how contagious is now the wisdom which builds churches and schools, and multiplies clergymen and schoolmasters, and gives Manchester a show such as monarchs cannot command? Wisdom honoured by nature, rewarded by the crown of long life and great happiness, or great reputation —for, if it give not these, it is not wisdom—has, in the long run, many more followers than folly with its jingling bells and its perishable though gaudy cap. A Locke, a Newton, or a Watt makes many generations of wise men, but the triflers, who invent or import grotesque customs, such as that of the huge wig under which our fashionable forefathers hid their heads, though universally followed for a brief season even by wise men,* are soon utterly forgotten. The fools, indeed, always have successors who will, in like manner, be very influential for their insect-hour, but the wise men continually live in our memories, and help to mould posterity in their own sublime forms.

Than this silent influence thus familiarly illustrated, which makes children like their parents, pupils like their teachers, and men like their associates, which gives to the members of every community qualities peculiar to themselves, and extends throughout society, there is nothing of more importance in reference to the general morality or our special criminality. Believing it to be, in contradistinction to much hollow plastering by laws and regulations and constrained education, the real cement of society which binds firmly together this multifarious mosaic, making it the most wonderful work out of heaven, allow me to delay you by one or two additional illustrations of its effects.

On the 8th of August last, it was stated, in an evening

* Though the common portrait of Locke, prefixed to his works, is without a wig, both Locke and Newton, I believe, conformed to the custom of their time, and covered their heads with nasty perukes.

paper, as a curious circumstance, that the number of convictions for juvenile delinquency in Aberdeen had risen from 8 in 1851 to 49 in 1854, the chief cause of which was that the receivers of stolen goods had imitated the Aberdeen Industrial Feeding Schools ; feeding, clothing, and lodging the children they could catch, and showing them where they could thieve. In imitation of reformatories, training schools for the purpose of initiating and improving thieves in their profession, and preparing them to carry it on with profit and safety to themselves and to their employers, were established, " creating," says the journal, " a supply of juvenile delinquents as surely as a demand creates a supply of cotton or corn." Must we not smile at the vanity which altogether overlooks its own example, and hopesto promote what it desires by doing something, of which the consequences inevitably are what it wishes to avoid.

Passing, however, to more general facts, I observe, that all men gratify similar desires in a manner somewhat similar. They all breath, eat and drink, see and hear, shiver from cold, and seek the protection of a cave or a palace, and clothe themselves in skins, woolens, silks, or furs. They glow equally in the heat, and lay themselves down under the shady tree or court the cooling breeze in the open verandah. Even after they have made railways and raised balloons, they all alike use their legs to walk, and their hands to perform the labour to which, however great be knowledge and skill, all are doomed. Even those who are supposed to live in idleness, have at least to labour to get and secure in their own possession the fruits of productive industry. But, conjoined with all thesegreat necessities, the silent influence adverted to, modifies perception, disposition, passions, motives, conduct, and helps to impress and to preserve on the individuals of each family, and each community, peculiar characteristics.

Man is born in society as he is born a human being. Laws do not create it. He is gregarious like the sheep ; and, like the bee works in common to procure his own and the general sustenance. Social industry is one great whole. Food may come from Egypt, the raw materials of manufacture from Georgia, and both may be the produce of a slave who never heard even the name of England. Without knowing it, certainly without always reflecting on it, we all live in mutual and reciprocal dependance, which becomes more manifest and more stringent as population, carrying with it division of labour, increases. In this condition of mutual dependance, society would only be a succession of conflicts, rubbing itself to pieces, were not men endowed with the means of moulding one another by a reciprocal and silent action; so that all serve the common end of promoting the general welfare.

Under this silent influence, we take our meals in company at the same hours, which preserves order and saves time. We consume very generally too, similar substances, some of which, brought from afar, extend the mutual dependance and brotherhood of humanity. At first, the use of such commodities was the highly-prized luxury of one or a few, and their silent influence, or the spirit of imitation, made these commodities the daily sustenance of the many. If we know not when sugar first came into use, the fathers of the oldest amongst us might almost remember when tea and coffee became the daily drink of the people, and all know that the use of them has, of late years, much increased. Only in modern times have they been imported in large quantities, and now we consume annually more than eight million cwts. of sugar, sixty million pounds of tea, and thirty-five million pounds of coffee. The use of these articles, beginning with a few, has been latterly accompanied, in deference to the silent influence of the upper classes, who have become more sober than their fathers, by more sobriety in the multitude and a proportionable improvement in the manners and habits of all.

A great, but an unfounded, outcry is made by a large party, more conspicuous for self-seeking than wisdom, against the increasing drunkenness of the people. You will not, therefore, be displeased, I hope, to learn from the metropolitan police reports, that the number of cases of drunkenness and disorder which fell under the notice of the police was, in 1831, 41,736, and of these 9,724 were summarily convicted. In 1832 the number taken up was 37,636, and convicted 5,682. Subsequent to this last period the area over which the jurisdiction of the police extended was much enlarged, and the amount of population within the area was every year very much increased. If drunkenness had increased, or even if it had continued to be as great as formerly, the number of drunken cases should have increased very much. But the fact is, that in 1855 the number was only 22,396, of which 7,751 were summarily convicted; and in 1856, a year of disbanded militia and great outrages, the number of cases of drunkenness and disorder taken cognizance of by the metropolitan police, in the largely increased population of a much larger area, was 21,805, and of these 7,674 were summarily convicted. A very decided proof that the people have improved in sobriety, though it is also a very decided proof that much more improvement is required. How to bring it about is between the enthusiastic partizans of Neal Dow or the Maine Liquor Law, and the common-sense supporters of anti-coercion, a question much in dispute.

Taking meals regularly and uniformly has another advantage. It ensures the regular and equal recruitment of the body, and avoids alike, the severe hunger and gorging which are attributes of the savage. It gives us a corresponding equanimity of temper, and saves the civilized man from the terrible anger of the hungry and slothful apathy of the over-sated man. It seems to be followed also by longer life. Great changes result from this silent influence combined with the necessity to eat. One person finds out the advantages of regular habits, or the pleasure of using non-intoxicating drinks; his practice influences the conduct of others, it forms the habits of multitudes, and of many generations, and imparts new qualities and new characteristics to human nature.

The necessity to protect ourselves against the inclemencies of the seasons does not lead us to clothe ourselves so much alike that the maid cannot be distinguished from the mistress, nor the man from the master; nor does it induce us to build our houses in one almost uniform manner or with slight deviations, dictated by individual fancies. These effects are the result of the silent influence of one man over another, combined with the general laws which determine the production of commodities; and the changes in dress and buildings, in time and place, which ensue and extend over a whole people, become memorials and marks of epochs in the history of every long-lived nation.

"There is a physiognomy in houses," said the "New York

Tribune," of October 14th, 1856, "as well as in their masters, and the architecture of an age or country generally tells by its features and their expression the stage of civilisation that demands it. The Greeks built their temples reverently, and slighted none of their work because it would *not be seen of men*—for, as they said, 'The gods see everywhere.' So the ecclesiastical architects of the middle ages, when the sacred poems were composed by them in stone, which are an astonishment and a despair to their successors, wrought in an elevated and religious spirit, which yet speaks to us from the walls of York, of Westminster, and of Antwerp. So with the domestic edifices of all times—they tell of the civilisation of the age they mark. Where nothing but the palace remains, we may be sure that the 'common rout,'

'Heads without name, no more remembered,'

were housed in hovels which perished with them and left no vestige behind. The castles of the dark ages tell of the uncertainty of life and havings which they were built to guard against. *And the gradual springing up of manor-houses and country-seats, at first with moats, which have long since been turned into flower-gardens, and with drawbridges, long dropped for ever, prove the growing safety to body and estate which left leisure and means for the comforts of civilised habitations.* And so of town and city architecture. *Peace and security made palaces for merchant princes, and solid dwellings for substantial burghers grow out of the land or out of the sea to tell the story of their golden days.*

"The churches and houses of the American cities are also expressive of the character of the people that worship in the one and live in the other. *The desire of making the greatest display possible of the wealth invested in these constructions, leads to the shallow hypocrisies of our temples,* and the thin pretensions of our houses. A church, apparently of solid granite or freestone, points the way to heaven with a spire of sanded wood, and when you turn the corner you see the coarse brick substance of the empty show in front—like a priest wearing a rough working-dress under the exterior magnificence of his robes. And the massive stone fronts of the wealthier sort of houses, which would persuade you that they will endure as long as the palaces of Venice, show you at the edges that their glory and their eternity are but of a handsbreadth."*

The contrast between a Chatsworth and the cabin of a Celt, or one of those primitive thatched styes yet seen in some parts of England, may suggest to us how wide and ever increasing, but for the silent influence of example, would be the difference between the fate of fortunate and unfortunate families. In the progress of society, education, leisure, different pursuits, necessarily confining the attention of each to different objects, all tend to make knowledge various and habits conflicting ; and this silent influence is the oil which lessens and destroys the friction of dissimilar individuals and dissimilar classes. The practices of one are imitated by another. Enjoyments are continually equalized. The toe of the peasant is for ever galling the kibe of the courtier. Chatsworth has many rivals, or like Stowe or Fonthill, it may crumble down to the common proportions. No individual, and no class, can, under this dispensation, secure a monopoly of enjoyment, advantage, or power. There is a constant tendency to revert to the original equality of mankind, and always to preserve it, while all are improved.

From the universality of changes, such as I have adverted to, it is plain that they are not the results of chance or individual fancies. In fact, they are *necessary consequences* of our instincts and our mutual influence over one another, which has been known as long as man has been in existence. We find, too, when the question is examined, that this necessity is embodied in a material form. The influence of the upper classes over the dress of the multitude, already mentioned, illustrates this necessity. The power they possess over the resources of society necessarily leads manufacturers who desire to share their wealth to study their inclinations, and adapt the productions of the loom to their use or their taste. What comes thus much into use can be made cheaply, and hence what is first made to suit the upper classes, gradually becomes the necessity of others. Accordingly, throughout Europe the various old costumes of the lower

* These remarks of the spirited journalist fell under my notice after my own opinions were put on paper.

classes and of the peasantry are everywhere disappearing, or rather are driven away by what may be called Paris modes and town manufactures. In our advanced country peculiar costumes, except some convenient dresses for particular classes of workers, have entirely disappeared. The bulk of the peasantry can find no other clothing than that made for the townspeople. Thus dress, which seems inconvenient to the multitude, which at least is not the most convenient nor the most graceful they could adopt, is, in a manner, forced on them.

Every season the cast-aside fashions of the upper classes become bargains for the multitude, and are readily adopted. The fashions of the drawing-room, or some imitation of them, descend from the drawing-room to the street; and almost every active and bustling woman is now an example that the influence of others is more powerful than her own personal interest, or even her own graceful appearance. We all, in truth, think far less of ourselves than how we appear in the sight of others, and are all obliged, as is much complained of by certain strong-minded individuals, to sacrifice self to conventionalities. This influence of the upper classes over dress and all the minute business of our lives excite a suspicion that the domestic defects now complained of in the women of the lower classes is in a great measure due to the example of ladies rather than to any mere deficiency of school training. High-born dames, and those who imitate them as a rule, not merely neglect household management, but speak of it with contempt as household drudgery. By their example and their language they teach those beneath them to despise it. In all the advertisements of finishing seminaries there is much said about accomplishments, and not a word about household management. When ladies of distinction return to the old practice of keeping the keys, looking after the preserves and the linen, and doing the duties of good housewives, the working classes will not be long unable to find a poor man's wife. They must remember that do as I teach and not as I do, may be a pleasant rule, but it is not a correct one, for their deeds will be necessarily imitated, while their teaching may blow past as the idle wind.

Let me further remind you of the general system of drainage and the removal of exuviæ, on which depends to some extent the health of all. In my younger days water-closets, with close-shutting valves, were unknown. They are as yet butlittle used on the Continent. At first they were very costly, and were exclusively erected in the houses of the opulent, carrying away all the feculent matter into the public sewers, maintained by a common rate, while the rest of the people were still put to the expense and nuisance of night-carts. Others next in the scale of opulence, from the cleanliness, the convenience, and cheapness, of course adopted the plan. As the invention came more into use, it became cheaper and extended faster to the lower strata of society. The very business by which the multitude were served came to an end, and a practice introduced almost within my memory has become a matter of necessity for every family in the metropolis. The legislature has recognised it, and compels the owners and builders of houses, to provide a water-closet for every one, communicating with the common drain. Individuals can have no choice about the matter; and this case is an illustration of the important general fact, that what is first adopted by one, or a few influential persons, for their ease, convenience, or gratification, very generally becomes a stern and unavoidable necessity for the multitude.

Then as to meat: the opulent classes buy the prime joints, and the coarser pieces would be wasted unless the lower classes could buy and consume them. This occurs. The coarse meat becomes the chief meat the poor can get, and thus their diet, sorry though it continue to be, as the diet of the upper classes is improved, necessarily becomes better. A similar fact is observed as to bread. In England wheaten bread has, as the general rule, replaced the barley bread and oaten cakes which were still the chief food of the people of the North of England in my youth. At present the better sort of cereals, or fine wheaten bread, are displacing the coarser sort—the black rye bread, the pumpernickel that is still common in many parts of the North of Europe. How the change is brought about is plain. The opulent, borrowing the taste perhaps from other countries, prefer wheaten bread, French rolls, &c., to the bread commonly consumed by the multitude. The cultivators find it for their interest to grow an increased quantity of the finer cereal. In favourable years the quantity thus grown exceeds the limited demand, and then it becomes proportionably cheaper than the coarser cereals. It is offered to the lower classes; they acquire a taste for it, and thus they are driven by this kind of necessity—cheapness in the end governing us all—to live on better bread.

So as to drink. We have already seen how the luxuries of the rich as to tea and coffee have become in a manner the necessities of the multitude. It is notorious that the extended use of these articles has been brought about by their cheapness combined with their agreeableness in reference to other drinks, When the government stood in the way of the extended use by mischievous customs duties, it lessened or abolished them, and then the people used the articles more freely. As to spirituous drinks the case was not different. The use of them from the time of the patriarchs began with the upper classes. To drink wine and strong drink was the delight of Norman and Saxon chiefs, and for many years the boast and pride, as well as the delight of our nobility and gentry. The people imitated them, but being unable to command the best drinks naturally took to the cheapest. Skilful distillers supplied their wants, and gin, on which a man could get drunk for 2d., was publicly advertised. The multitude imitated as best they could the example of barons, priests, and squires, and till these latter saw their own orgies reflected in all the hideous aggravation of gin, they were not aware of their folly, and the mischief it effected. With their accustomed ignorance and love of coercion, they began, when they became aware of it, to punish the multitude for the vice they had engendered.

Individuals are continually blamed for excessive expenditure, but very often this is as much the result of necessity as any of the habits I have alluded to. Every person is born in a certain rank in Europe, as he is born in a caste in Hindostan, and as he born in society. He is compelled to remain in that rank, or he desires to remain in it, or to rise above it. In either case he must conform to the expenditure of a class. To keep in the rank in which a man was born, or to move in another, a certain expenditure is necessary, and whether a man have the means or not, only by the expenditure which distinguishes classes can he enter or continue in a class. This is but another term for continuing in society, and thus a proper expenditure and the most extreme frugality are to certain classes as necessary as air.

We trace the same predominating influence in morals. In England a man must swallow his saliva; in the United States he squirts it out for pastime, and encourages the secretion for the enjoyment. In Italy, where suspicion—growing from a great system of teaching lies—generally prevails, a tailor will not part with the clothes he has made to order, unless the money be handed over with one hand as the clothes are received by the other. Barter has returned to the country in the wake of fraud, where credit was first systematised. In Italy credit is little known, here it is the basis of most transactions. Future production depends very much on credit, on what men hope to get more than on what they have already got. Hence the delayed progress of Italy and its deficient prosperity are due to the want of credit, and this again is due to the fradulent teaching of its rulers. If we should be obliged by our fraudulent leaders of various kinds, like the Italians, to fall back on barter, we should soon tread the downward path to national decay. Individuals cannot but conform to social customs, and those who contribute to form them are rarely sensible how much depends upon their often careless conduct.

We inherited sailing ships, turnpike-roads, and stage-coaches from our predecessors, and were as much compelled to adopt and to use them in order to subsist as we are compelled to eat and to breathe. This generation, however, has invented steam-boats and railways, and for making voyages or journeys we are all now obliged to use them. They are the best and cheapest conveyances known. So all the new and pleasant inventions of one generation, its choice apparently, which might, some persons think, not have been chosen, become the necessities of its successors. This is equally true of moral obligations as of physical constraints. The criminals of the present time are the offspring of past errors. Like railroads and steam-boats they are our necessities, the direct consequences, probably, of penal laws, the national debt, locked up land, a fettered commerce, an extravagant government, and an established church. The rule therefore, that "at Rome you *must* do as they do at Rome," holds generally good, and the *morality of the multitude*, like their dress and the drainage, is derived, by a species of constraint from others who punish them for the peculiarities they have at least been instrumental in introducing.

I have expatiated at great length on the mutual influence of man on man, to show how widely diffused is its operation; now I must say a few words on its intensity. It makes the soldier brave death and the suicide rush into eternity. The love of glory and the fear of infamy are only this influence concentrated by the voice of ages into one overwhelming emotion, which often masters the strongest of our animal passions.

In the case of national war, it sets aside all moral sentiments, and all the teaching of religion, and makes men rush on self-destruction, while they deal out death, or commit the murder they are taught to abhor, at the command of a political authority respected at present, far less from the convictions of reason than from the sentiments they have inherited.

"Abstract," says the most philosophic of our poets—

> "Abstract what others feel, what others think,
> All pleasures sicken, and all glories sink."

This influence is, therefore, a powerful means of moulding character, void of the offensiveness and cruelty of gaols and gibbets. Can it not, then, be used instead of them to repress the crimes which now torment us; and, if we are tormented by crimes, are not those in fault who, being endowed with wonderful power, use it, ignorantly and ineffectually, for the repression of crimes.

Day after day elaborate leading articles are written in the newspapers, with some hope to influence the policy of our own or other governments. They hold up, as an example, some former policy, or the present policy of some other nations. Hardly any thing politically new is ventured on, and all that is recommended has succeeded, or is succeeding elsewhere. Such articles being written under a conviction that they will influence some minds, my brother journalists are tacit advocates of the opinion that the influence man exercises over man by persuasion and example is all powerful for good or for evil. If it can model national policy, as is implied in every journal, it cannot be without influence on national character. If our example as a nation, enforced by our newspapers, can produce indignation in the people of Europe at restraints imposed on the press,—which must, in the end, either achieve its freedom or destroy the governments which restrict it,—cannot the example of our upper classes produce and establish honour and honesty at home? If the growth of opinion, founded on fact, be strong enough to put down religious intolerance and political tyranny, it must be strong enough to sweep away for ever the pocket-picking, and the breaches of trust, with all their kindred offences, and the whole present prevalent and shameful system of preying on one another. But this system, begun in old oppression and wrong, is maintained by the privileged and endowed classes. It may be traced in every importunate demand of royal and other societies to be provided for out of the property of individuals, miscalled the public money, the public or state having no money but what it takes from individuals. It is incorporated in most of our laws; and its general prevalence among the multitude is due like most of their habits to the example of their leaders. As long as it lasts punishments to repress theft will be of no avail, and till the upper classes set the example of respecting the property of the multitude, they will continue to be tormented by frauds and thefts.

The influence adverted to is altogether social; a perfectly and always solitary being can know nothing of it. Like many other parts of society, like division of labour and exchange, it grows and becomes intense as society extends. By the same means, the dependence of each individual on the mass, is continually augmented, and the importance of any one to the whole, however skilful, wise, and powerful, is diminished. Each one is subjected, as society advances, more completely, mind and body, to all the others. This influence, or this great fact, could only be properly appreciated, even if earlier known, in modern times as society has developed, and as interchange has knit together the most distant people, knocking down the boundaries of those municipal laws and national institutions on which each has relied more than on the laws of nature, for the prevention of crime. Perhaps you noticed in the debate before the late dissolution, that our authorities at Hong Kong, according to their despatches, and our representatives in the House of Commons, displayed great eagerness to obtain the good opinion of the

Chinese. They shelled the town of Canton to make the Cantonese believe that they were superior to Yeh. They would have their love, if possible, if not, they would inspire them with dread. To obtain influence over Asiatics, we are obliged, according to General Williams and others, to become Asiatics in morals and principles. Evil communications corrupt good manners, and communicating with Asiatics and desiring to have influence over them, makes some amongst us forget their birth-place and the principles of freedom.

As contradistinguised from material, the influence is entirely mental. It is communicated from mind to mind by the medium of the external world; not like stripes and fetters from body to body. It is the very opposite to the cruel system of personal coercion, and without being irritating and disgusting, is all-efficient. Increasing in intensity as society increases,—matured and directed, if not wholly and entirely generated by its growth, it seems exactly adapted to tame and modify individual passions, volitions and motives, and quietly bring them all into harmony with the general interests. It is strengthened and developed by all the exertions now continually made by education and otherwise to give predominancy to the mental element of our being, while the practice of constraining or torturing the body promotes, in opposition to all these exertions and to the course of society, the predominancy of sensual and bodily pains, with their accompaniments, violent and ill-regulated emotions. This silent and mutual influence must be the foundation of every righteous system of laws, intended, like the laws of nature, to unite all men by the principle of mutual service and mutual respect for each other's rights. Our present penal system separates men, and separates classes. It is in essence a slave-code directed against the poor. It enacts injuries and violates rights ; proceeding to the extraordinary and absurd conclusion of torturing and destroying life, in order to make life safe and agreeable.

Mural tablets recorded, and civic crowns encouraged, virtue in ancient Greece; but these and similar methods of obtaining useful and just ends are neglected by our legislative classes, who prefer the old barbarity of torturing the body to informing the mind. Legions of Honour, Stars and Garters, Golden Fleeces, Orders of the Lion and the Sword have, indeed, been invented to serve the purposes of Governments, not of morality, and have been prostituted to strengthen the motives which degrade men into servile courtiers, or render them skilful as gluttonous destroyers. On this all-important means of promoting their own welfare, men have, in modern times at least, pretended to give up the right of private judgment: and even give up their property in morality. They have permitted the wealth which should foster honesty, to be wasted on princely corruption and priestly fraud. They have lavished the natural income of virtue on folly and vice. The means which should improve the heart of humanity, goes to bedizen corrupt governments and barbarous superstition. Not merely the vulgar, who delight in Royal processions and Lord Mayors' shows, but the men of mark in society who aspire to be its leaders, are to blame for this. Both by their teaching and their example they idolize stars, and ribands, and titles, and make an enthroned scamp the judge of human merit, and the dispenser of rewards. If any thing palpable, or of which we are conscious, deserves the name of the soul of society, it is the mutual moral influence we exercise over one another; and if any thing deserves the name of grasping ambition in rulers and servility in subjects, it is the permitted assumption and perversion of this influence to the purposes of misgovernment. If any centralization and monopoly of authority be more outrageous and destructive of morality than another, it is the implicit surrender to authority of the right of bestowing rewards and honours. By it, men are induced to struggle, not to serve their fellows, but to obtain the favour of kings and ministers. For the virtues which bless, we nourish the vices which curse society. From such a terrible sacrifice in matters spiritual our Protestant forefathers emancipated us, and in matters secular we must now emancipate ourselves. We have the power. In spite of a supposed delegation to Government, and in spite of its usurpation, it is impossible for individuals to denude themselves of their mutual influence. Hence journalists and the public, while they nominally profess the utmost reverence for Government, continually sit in judgment on its acts; and, in spite of the nobility or the riband it bestows, they dub the lord an ass, and the general a bungler or a coward. Its decorations only deceive the vulgar, and cannot shield the unworthy man they cover from contempt.

In the class of influential persons who sometimes make at least a careless use of this great means of moulding men into honesty, journalists must be included. Like the Levites of old, they are the expounders of the law and guides of opinion; they influence those who are nominally the leaders of society. By the foremost of them it was stated, a few months ago, "It is of no consequence how a man is rewarded." It is, therefore, of no consequence on what the approbation or the censure of the *Times* is bestowed. Day after day, accordingly, column after column is devoted to describe the ceremonies of a consecration; and paragraph after paragraph holds up to admiration my Lord the Bishop and the Right Rev. Dean; they are continually described as the salt of society; they preserve it on earth and prepare it for heaven; and having thus raised a great flutter of reverence in the bosoms of all the Mauds and Evangelines of the fashionable world, the *Times* mocks, with withering sarcasms, the loving testimonials its disciples bestow on "Leo Manybuttons, the High-Church Curate of St. Silvester in the Tiles," and the Low-Church Vicar, "the Rev. Eneas McGrowl." Journalists, as well as maidens, indulge in "silly effusions of unripe and ill-directed sentimentalism;" and continually squander the great moral inheritance of this generation. Our knowledge-born emotions it is their especial province to guard and wisely direct.

Before I explain in detail how the upper classes, by the means of their unavoidable influence, create most of the crimes committed against property, I am desirous of doing justice to their influence in lessening crimes of violence. Amongst them, though unjust appropriation is common, murder is now unknown. They never take life except by law, and they mark their disapprobation of the deed by branding the executioner with dishonour. No one of them, on any conditions, would be a hangman. They are under no temptation, except for the preservation of political power, to hedge their persons round with cruel laws as they hedge round property, and except laws for the repression of sedition and treason, they have taken no particular care, by legislation, of their own persons. They outrage no popular feeling, and make no war against any class when they decree death for murder, and try to check lawless by lawful violence. In all their personal intercourse they are duly sensible that violence begets violence. They have banished it accordingly from their daily lives. They eschew as vulgar all strong emotions, even to a little honest enthusiasm. Those amongst them who would forge bills, cheat on the race-course, or appropriate to their personal use legacies left to the poor, hold it to be a scandal not to preserve an unruffled temper. It is their pride to be in their demeanour meek and mild as doves. In repressing violent emotions, their example has been efficacious, and its influence may be traced in our public meetings, and in our literature, as well as in our statistics. Intemperate language is every where curbed. To their habitual self-command, their suavity and gentleness, much of the general courtesy of society, but not all, is to be attributed, as well as the general diminution of crimes of violence to which I have called your attention. I may even say they are tenderly careful of each other, as the general rebuke which the class gave to Sir Robert Peel for his somewhat coarse allusions to the Prince de Ligné illustrates, though this occurred after the subject had engaged my thoughts.

Whatever they be to tenants, servants and labourers, to one another—all being, as the rule, alike free and equal, and all mutually exposed to the corrections of one another—they are essentially and strictly just. They may bilk a tradesman, but they pay their debts of honour. In their dealings one with another they are frank and open. In this sense their virtues are cosmopolitan. All sovereigns are brothers or cousins wherever they may reign. All the nobles of the different kingdoms of Europe are similarly related, and everywhere treat each other with a deference, politeness, and courtesy, they do not always show in their own countries to peasants, artizans, labourers and tradesmen. To produce amongst them—not in one country only, not exclusively in England, or in France, or in Spain, but in every country of Europe—mutual forbearance in their intercourse, and mutual politeness, if not mutual kindness, their mutual equality, and mutual freedom, are quite sufficient. They need no other, and have had no other coercion than the restraint which an equality of retort or resistance has everywhere imposed on all. Though I cannot exonerate them from the charge of continuing hereditary injustice to their so-called inferiors, I must say their polite or forbearing conduct towards one another, and their mutual and reciprocal respect are, for all, and even for themselves in their relation to their inferiors, an admirable example. If, in other lands, the upper classes might be supposed to be made of different clay from that of the common people, no such supposition is true of our own nobility and gentry, whom we see rising and know to have arisen from the mass, and to be one with it in blood. Why, then, should not the influence, which is all-sufficient to mould them, be equally sufficient to mould all, and make us all, properly directed, the most serviceable possible to one another—the sum of all social virtues.

The influence of the upper classes for good, however, does not end here. The general progress begins with some individual. If pioneers in the wilderness of wants had not commenced to solace themselves with the enjoyment of tea, it could not have become the general means of sobriety and the general cheerer of toil ; nor would its use in Europe have promoted the common civilization of the most distant members of the human family. Fine linen, the imperial purple, and the royal silk brocade, introduced as the exclusive dress of the idle and luxurious few, have become the comfortable clothing for all—needful for health, strength, and cleanliness. For the cultivation of the fine arts and literature, for judicious improvement in dress, still much needed both in point of convenience and ornament, there must be leisure and wealth. Science, too, is necessary. Society requires look-out men and pilots as well as working hands. The upper classes are the former.

Nor is this the only way in which our daily life is deeply indebted to their opulence. The means of subsistence must be easily obtained before the man finds a family a source of enjoyment. The woman and her child are one ; she cannot deny maternity, but there is no similar identity between the child and the father. Difficulties in the way of procuring subsistence always have been, from the very beginning of society to our own times, great obstacles to the performance of the duties of paternity. A man struggling for a bare subsistence, on the verge of starvation, cannot think of honour and happiness to be derived from children. He has no name to transmit, and can anticipate no fame reflected from his offspring. The opulence of some, though obtained at the expense of others, made it a pleasure for some fathers to protect and cherish their children, and laid the foundation for those paternal virtues, for which nature seems otherwise, by the absence of any strict bond between the child and the father, to have made but scant provision. The preference of beauty, too, in those who have full liberty of choice and ample means to gratify their inclination, tends to ennoble the race. The superiority of a few, therefore, which has always existed, seems necessary, if not for the continuance, for the increase and improvement of the species. They are the heralds of civilization. If all who are endowed with wealth and leisure, neither understand nor fulfil their functions, and if many not so endowed have heroically fought out the great battle of life, and have been affectionate, tasteful, elegant and enjoying, as well as courageous combatants, nevertheless, in the order of nature, who now, as at the beginning, is continually giving society leaders in heroic improvers, such are their functions, and the more strongly we are convinced of their influence for good, the more must they be blamed for all the evil which exists in society. Now, too, I am happy to say, they are becoming sensible of this. They are conscious of their great responsibility, but I am here also to say that they yet misunderstand the means by which alone they can fulfil their duty.

Even as to lessening crimes of violence, I cannot wholly acquit them of the charge of being negligent or ignorant. Had they discouraged the taking away life under any pretext, instead of ordaining it for numerous offences almost infinitely small compared to the death they decreed—had they, instead of sending men forth to slay each other, teaching them that suicide and murder are virtues, in obedience to a political expediency which subsequent events have convinced us was a mere fancy or a folly—had the upper classes discouraged, politically and nationally, hanging and war as much as they have discouraged violence in their personal intercourse, there can be no doubt, life is naturally so sanctified to the imagination, that taking it away on any occasion or on any pretext, would be dreaded and abhorred throughout society, and be almost unknown. But for a false political theory, ascribing to the state, in its corporate capacity, and therefore irresistible, a right which belongs to no one of the individuals composing it, except at the moment when his own safety is endangered, the right of killing in self-defence, which no individual ever resigns or can transfer to the public*—but for this false theory, which has led the upper classes continually to violate the right of life, using the power and the name of the community, the

* Feb. 11th. Only a few days ago, a youth was acquitted in Edinburgh, on a charge of homicide, who had slain a man in what he supposed was self-defence.

taking away life, in any case, would probably be more inconceivable than a bloody brawl amongst titled chamberlains in the Queen's drawing-room, or the presence of a high-bred lady, not insane, in her night clothes at a fashionable ball.

I have now pointed out in detail the intimate connection, moral and mental, which exists between all the individuals and all the classes in society, meaning it to be inferred, that the classes which take the lead in what they suppose to be good, and which is really civilization, are also responsible for much existing evil the consequence of pre-barbarism maintained by them, not, as is continually alleged, of advancing civilization.

All changes, whether for good or for evil, necessarily originate in some one mind, however ready may be contiguous minds to explode by the same spark. From one the spiritual communication—be it slow or rapid, take what prompting shape it may, of religion, or peculiarity of speech, or dress, or wild adventure, or steady mechanical progress—spreads through all classes and degrees, and gives a permanent development to society. The select few who first catch the light of coming knowledge, cannot use their advantages without passively, on their part, communicating a knowledge of them to others. As it is caught and diffused by imitation through the mass, it hardens into a feature of society, and is not only transmitted from indidividual to individual, but from age to age, and nation to nation. One cannot go far ahead of another. A glance over the history of Europe, the only history known with tolerable accuracy, informs us that its different people have passed through similar stages of thraldom and superstition, of ignorance and barbarism, to emerge at somewhat different periods, one always influencing the other into a similar condition of freedom, religion, knowledge, and humanity. They all share, more or less, in science which is one, and in arts which are almost universal. They are all, more or less, agricultural, manufacturing, and commercial, use nearly all the same measures of time, and the same metals as money, dividing them much in the same manner. They all trade with one another, and weigh their goods much alike by similar instruments, the balance being in use in almost all lands, though different people give different names to their measures and weights, and do not always make them correspond to the same quantities. They are always progressing together, borrowing science and art from one another, the least advanced being continually improved, though, as impatient politicians sometimes think, much too slowly, by the example of the foremost. They have all gone through pretty nearly the same moral phases. Especially, this is remarkable in the decrease of violent crimes, adverted to at the commencement of the Lecture. They *were* in a condition in which respect for life was not much greater than at present in China, or by the Sultans recently visited by our African travellers; they *are* in a condition in which homicide is scarcely tolerated for the presumed advantage of the State, or the security of the most revered authority. They have all, therefore, been morally developed, and are developing under the influence of similar laws. At every stage in this development, the morality of the mass has been, and is, mainly determined, like their fashions, by their leaders.

In modern times, the progress and assimilation have been very remarkable. Railroads, telegraphs, and photography, the inventions of yesterday, are already in use throughout the civilized world, compelling legislators to alter their policy, and giving an unmistakable uniformity of pursuit and character, of knowledge and art, to all the people of Europe.

About twenty centuries elapsed between the period when Rome made highways through all her Italian dominions, and the period when England first drove a great road through the highlands of Scotland. Now railroads, which were invented only a quarter of a century ago, are common to Europe and the United States. They are constructed in India, and will soon unite the Mediterranean, traversing Asia, with the Indian Ocean. Thus usefully, surely, and powerfully does the silent influence of example—and all the more swiftly and powerfully from being wholly disconnected from any and every kind of exhortation, command, or coercion—spread social improvements, which are moral improvements, effected by the instrumentality of mind, throughout every part of communicating society.

Born of our common mother, the earth—for man is emphatically dust, and always mutually connected with her, she bearing us all, as it were, for ever in her spacious womb, and always preserving us mentally united by the similar knowledge and similar impressions she produces in all—correcting, too, by invariable laws or by facts all our vague dreams, our inflated hopes, and our boundless imginations, false only because she does not confirm them ; united by and in her, the whole of mankind forms mentally but one family. The knowledge gathered by each is generally diffused, and as it is increased and comes to bear a larger predominating proportion over individual peculiarities, it constitutes one mind for all—imparting a great meaning to a couplet which you have, perhaps, often repeated as merely beautiful and impressive :—

> " All are but parts of one stupendous whole,
> Whose body Nature is, and God the soul."

This principle gives us the theoretical or abstract explanation o. the manner in which crimes—our present thefts—and virtues —our patriotic energy—become and continue national. As individuals, as classes, and as the incorporated state, we can indulge no desire, prosecute no action, practise no virtue nor crime, and enact no law which, in its visible effects, is not very influential in moulding the characters and minds of all. We can only make fitting laws, therefore, for great communities, which now constitute not merely a few hundred or thousand persons, not merely a few tribes, but many millions of men, of various lineage and various faiths, by ascertaining and fully comprehending the mutual and reciprocal influence exercised by the acts and the example of all the individuals and classes who compose them. We can only comprehend, too, the great subject of crime, by discarding municipal limits and institutions, and even national prejudices, and by extending our views past all human legislation to the great laws which establish an eternal distinction between right and wrong, and impose on every human being his or her own peculiar duties, and give him his own peculiar rights.

I stop now. I have found it impossible to condense into one lecture, even the leading principles of this great subject. I have rather indicated than fully explained them, and have left wholly untouched the erroneous theory adopted by the legislature concerning the right of property, and the actions of the ruling classes proceeding from it, which I regard as the chief sources of the present crimes of the multitude against property. The attention you have kindly given to what I have now said, induces me to hope that you will honour me by your presence at another lecture, in which these important points, together with the only practical means suggested by experience, for effecting speedy and immediate improvement, will be explained in some detail.

APPENDIX.

SEE PAGE 19.

THE reader will probably be aware, however, that there are physiological facts which influence, if they do not determine exactly, the periods at which we should feed. "There is some reason, beyond mere custom," says Dr. Draper,* "which has led to the mode of distributing the daily meals. A savage may dispatch his gluttonous repast, and then starve for want of food; but the more delicate constitution of the civilized man, demands a more perfect adjustment of the supply to the wants of the system, and that, not only as respects the kind, but also the time. It seems to be against our instinct to commence the morning with a full meal. We breakfast, as it is significantly termed, but we do no more, postponing the taking of the chief supply until dinner, at the middle or after-part of the day. There are many reasons for supposing, when we recall the time which must elapse between the taking of food and the completion of respiratory digestion (the source of heat), that the distribution of the meals is not so much a matter of custom, as an instinctive preparation for the systematic rise and fall of temperature attending on the maxima and minima of daily heat. The light breakfast has a preparing reference to noonday, the solid dinner to midnight." The civilized man, in fact, requires a more equable and continual nourishment of the body than the savage; and the nutriment of all, not only as to its qualities, but as to hours of taking it, is regulated in some measure by external circumstances. The great necessity we are all under to eat in order to live, carries its laws into all the details of our lives, and affords in them an illustration of the fact, that civilisation is, in all its parts, as much matter of necessity as taking food. The conditions of life, I have elsewhere remarked, are changed, and life probably, we may, indeed, say certainly, has changed too. But life did not change itself, it is changed

---

* Human Physiology. Samson Low and Co.

by a superior power ; and, therefore, it is to be inferred that man, another name for a limited portion of life, did not, except as an instrument in the hands of a higher power, bring forward the civilization, on promoting some very unimportant portions of which certain classes lay a claim to wealth and power.

For every created animal and plant appropriate food is, at least at its commencement, provided. In eggs and milk, the sustenance necessary for the young, is duly prepared and laid up independently of the volition of the parents. For the origin and preservation of all animal life, therefore, including its highest type—man, the Creator has made a most careful and marked provision. The bearings of such a fact on the little respect we are accustomed to show to the bodies of our fellow-creatures, the instruments of life, and the wantonness and hasty rapacity with which we maim or destroy them, ought not be lost sight of. The life we disregard, it is the delight of the Great Lord and Creator of all, if we may attribute human emotion to him, to bestow and sustain. We can scarcely imagine that He can have made such a provision for the nutrition of infants and be wholly indifferent to the nutrition of the parents. The care, too, which He takes to provide food for infants, illustrates the necessity of men providing a good diet for themselves. The food of the people of Europe within recollection, and the food of all nations within the records of history, has been materially changed and improved. Physiologists tell us, that the general diet of the agricultural classes is not, in substance, very different from the general diet of all classes, consisting of bread, cheese, and beer, containing all the elements conducive to the sustenance of the bodily frame ; but the general use of the substances now referred to—tea, coffee, sugar, &c.—involves a great change in the diet of many nations. With this change in the diet there have been contemporaneous changes in the clothing of man. The body being, as the rule, everywhere maintained, and partly by diet, at the same temperature, requires clothing, and thus clothing and feeding the race are, at least, of as much importance as sustaining the life of a chick, or even as providing, in the mother's body, for the continual warmth of the yet unborn infant. Changes in the diet and clothing consequently—such as have passed under our own observation, and as we learn from history, have taken place at various periods—are not the unimportant matters which ascetic historians, who carefully chronicle war and censure luxury in dress, and legislators, who interfere to regulate or stint the diet of the people, would have us believe. They are ordered or prohibited results. If prohibited, we shall soon have that impressed on us by their evils. But the changes which have ensued in the diet and clothing of the people of Europe, subsequent to the discovery of the route to India by the Cape of Good Hope, far from being evil, have been accompanied by greater average longevity, by milder dispositions, by a diminution of some loathsome diseases and many serious crimes, and, generally, by those improvements or approximations to perfection which are denominated civilization. They are not, therefore, matters of indifference, or even of trifling importance; and, until other facts demonstrate that the present use of these varied kinds of food and clothing be evil, we must conclude that they are as much willed by our Great Creator, as the provision which *He* makes for the continued procreation and sustenance of animal life.

[Since this lecture was delivered, it has been distinctly proved, in the admirable report of the commissioners for inquiry into lunatic asylums in Scotland, that insanity is in many cases the result of poor and insufficient diet. What other testimony can be required to the necessity of the legislature abstaining, entirely and totally, from imposing any restrictions whatever on all the great businesses by which individuals or societies feed themselves.]

GROOMBRIDGE BROTHERS, PRINTERS, EXETER-STREET, STRAND.

www.ingramcontent.com/pod-product-compliance
Lightning Source LLC
LaVergne TN
LVHW052016160826
845678LV00003B/1075

* 9 7 8 0 3 5 3 2 8 3 6 0 2 *